Immigrant

STANLEY NELSON

IMMIGRANT

Book III

BIRCH
BROOK
PRESS

Other Books by Stanley Nelson
The Passion of Tammuz (Bellosguardo Press)
Idlewild (The Smith)
The Brooklyn Book of the Dead (The Smith)
Chirico Eyes (Midnight Sun)
The Travels of Ben Sira (The Smith)
The Unknowable Light of the Alien (The Smith)
101 Fragments of a Prayer (Midnight Sun)
Nightriffer (Birch Brook Press)
Driftin' on a Nightriff (Sub Rosa Press)
Immigrant Book I & II (Birch Brook Press)
Ode for Giorgio de Chirico (Pinched Nerve Press)

Designed & Printed at
Birch Brook Press
PO Box 81
Delhi, NY 13753
Hand Typesetting by Joyce Tolnay
Write for free catalog

To my wife, Betty Jean—
who joined me on
The Immigrant Quest

About the Author

IMMIGRANT III is the thirteenth book of poetry by Stanley
Nelson, and the fourth published by Birch Brook Press. The first
was NIGHTRIFFER published in 1985. A book of stories, THE
UNKNOWABLE LIGHT OF THE ALIENS (The Smith), was
named a Small Press Book of the Year by *Library Journal*. Nelson's
poems have appeared in such publications as *Triquarterly, Beloit
Poetry Journal, Kansas Quarterly, Confrontation, The Smith, For
Now, Turnstile,* and *Pinched Nerve*. His work has appeared in
several anthologies including *Longshot* and *Yearbook of American
Magazine Verse*.

Reverie 13

The Signal System provides safety and close spacing between trains for Rapid Transit operations. This is accomplished by installing the interconnecting thousands of components into a coordinated functioning system that in all phases stresses safety.

The heart of the Signal System is the Track Circuit. Lengths of track are sectionalized into signal blocks by insulated rail joints. The Track Circuit detects the presence or absence of a train in a signal block and by means of interconnected controls properly positions the automatic train stops and displays the proper signal aspects. A green aspect indicates to the motorman that the signal blocks ahead are clear and that it is safe to proceed at normal speed. A yellow aspect indicates to the motorman that the next signal will be displaying a red aspect and that he can proceed with caution and be prepared to stop at the next signal. A red aspect is a stop and stay indication which informs the motorman of the presence of another train on the signal blocks close ahead. All signals are provided with an automatic train stop to insure proper observance of the stop (red) indication of the signal. Any train attempting to pass a red signal is automatically brought to a stop by the tripping arm of the wayside automatic stop. In this manner, the Signal System protects the movement of all trains.

The Track Circuit is defined as a series of electrical circuits, of which rails of the track form an integral part. The track transformer feeds electrical energy into one end of the signal block, through the remaining rails to the track relay at the other end of the signal block. As long as electric current flows through this path, the track relay remains energized, indicating that no train is present in that signal block. When a train enters the block, its wheels and solid axle short the Track Circuit and cause the track relay to become de-energized. The other interconnected signal

circuits then cause the signal to display a red aspect and the
proper automatic stop to come to the tripping position.

slipped)   into Abyss

                    Childer

                              Mass   Maw

of Animus   Craw

                              of Dis   /and the grind of

          Evil pouches and the voice of grinders and the grinding
          paradiddle
          sudden to be thrown into the BMT

                    you can't get to heaven
                    on the BMT
                    cause the BMT

          will be emp-tee
          Father, the Darkness
          Mother, the Abyss

                                        muck

darkblooded region me
no mourning   air mother-me-
down the Abyss slipped
                              off-the-tilt
of the dreamtime, lost
that Aliensmudge forgot what
                    is the season?   what

time what is the time
please whereunto

have we been thrown?

O Adamantine Land

It is I, I, I descended to the midst of the
underworld and shone my darkness
down upon Darkness
a boundless darkness, water
of unfathomable depths

They made us go
bigmacher machomen
we didn't want to
We woke to alarm
threw away our baseball mitts,
stashed our bikes and skates out of harm's
way.   I became *you*, this became *It*
we became *they*.   lost lost
our aliensmudge, our eyes, lashes melt
ed in the heat that is not hot

nor cold, but is as it were
a vapor seeping excrementally
from rusted railcore.
and what we felt incrementally
the day before we feel
today—till bodyheat elementally
with other heat congeals
with flesh embondaged but outside
normal time.   on wheels
of stale fire our pasty substance rides.

Against the turnstile we lean
            gingerly as if against some wind
            unclaimable. we must be neat,
our clothes spic and span,
            our raincoat unspotted and folded
            crisply in the crook of the arm.
we have mastered this ritual
            of passing through the terminal ungrimed—
            as we have mastered the folding
of the early morning *Times*

into thirds. then we must stand
            elbows at our sides so as not to invade
            the aeon of a neighborform.
then too there is the briefcase
            always to be handled with aplomb
            so that the three—paper, folded rain
coat, briefcase—are soldered into one.
            the span of every morning begins at Bush
            Terminal, 36th Street, among hordes
in wary symbiosis just like us.

You can't get on *any* train, off and on
            at *any* stop: there is no time—choose
            RR or B or LL or KK or N—
not like taking any bus
            on sly slow afternoons. here time
            pulses on your wrist, slips
down to parts where no light
            gleams. choose: *your* train:
            there is no choice—you accept
its route-allotted timeframe, unvar

ying, this morn this eve eternally.

12

Listen! a B train! roaring
coneyward in opposite direction so we
can't get on. across the platform
through yellow separative tiles.
we see only the flare of wheels, scorch
of approach. There is no time.
we hear and we know and accept
wooosh of train that is our train
but sealed from unadept.

Finally it comes in stark
celebration, your northbound express.
you can't afford now that slow arc
of the local moving rapturous
to any station. where hardly anyone
gets off and on it stops, hums,
then toonervilles along—
obsolete cars half-filled
with characters who slouch and snore.
You're on the B; you're northbound; the local's

far from your recall. pressed hard
against the crowd—those of tonsured
mien, graffiti in their hearts—
you become the sullen monster
stalking shudderdreams and latenite
films. you are dead in your body;
your mind has appetite
only for graphs and schedules, xeroxes
of xeroxes, requisitions, reports,
vouchers, receipts—all that occurs

set down and stored in replicate.
Northward B wooshes out

13

to bay.   you do not look up.
you do not see in your heart
     there is no day, there is no sun,
     from the tunnel it roars and shouts
and sudden you are thrown onto
     bridge supports, burning toward
     the Place you vowed never to go
that is not our Place.   twinhulk mounds

Godzillaville.   stony hardons,
     schmutzbelch.   you are high, high
     above a river.   somewhere light reflects on
water.   but your grim eye
     catches only an edge of chiaroscuro
     arcing toward darkness, underside
of refuse and rotted piers.
     landfill: they have brought
     us, landfill, the Big Operators.
habitual in our bodystumps, we do not

look up.   ever.   for if our gaze
     should dare (in fixed guise) to glance
     above Godzillaville, this very veer
of sky—white gull entranced
     by white cloud, climbing sunburst,
     wind opening to bay and ocean—
sea and sky atwine and the river
     cleansed by currents primal—*such*
     pain would cleave our hearts.   better
to bow our heads in aversion

focusing on nothing with a look of null conformation
until the train blurs tunnelward in choleric purgation.   O

14

you can't get to heaven
on the subway car
cause the subway car
won't get that far

                              far

way

        past

Fost

        er
                furthesout
                Place: but

        we did, once,
        almost, come closest
        anyways, cept for that
        time on the Ferris wheel ac
        cepted into
                        Sky   in the slow time   dream

                        time   break

                                                        time
in that space between that other mode
of hopskotch jigsaw afternoons
and the squat aeon of transit maps
when the jigsaw, well, jigsawed, jugolinijed, fell
apart forever for
the rest of our lives
                        yet even the most sarkic

                    among us of cheerless

                                                        cast

swaying on the B in close array
briefly retraces   that
retraces   Other

                            mode

when we stood at peace
with palms up
utterly
entranced on any station of the El
watching sunlight filter wooden beams
of outdoor elevated platforms. (if it rains
you retreat to norman-arched panels).
never impatient, but playful, lots, lotsa time—
each day slow in its season—and *they* were different
back then, there were no overseers or archons. even the
                                            changebooth

woman was not unfriendly. she never smiled, true. but also
she never scowled. and she gave you change, change for the
                                            turnstile,
handfuls of silvery change—all the change you ever
wanted. Tokens? never heard of 'em. They were not so far
those days, from the summers people ordered pitchers of beer
on Autenreich's open porch. The conductor
told you directions
and tipped his jolly blue-peaked cap;
you never had to strive with subway maps
to mushroom into wads in your backpocket.
Turnstile: you went in and out the same one!
Entrance and exit the same! From where you were

                            16

where farms were idling to vacant lots
(the circus pitched its tents there) you boarded
when the train was near to empty. You never sat.
Just loitered by glass-panel doors or stood
on the small causeway between cars, gripping
the chains. the train was outside a long time
churning from one toonerville stop to another,
where hardly anyone gets on or off.

And you were outside too, gripping the chains
against wind. Even if you stood inside
by the doors you could still *feel* outside—
the way backyard trees bunched
between clotheslines, feel and mood
of playground swings, faraway haze
of bridges. when it varoomed
to where two rivers verge on bay and ocean,
then rollercoasted toward the tunnel,
you were ready. you ran to the first car

and grabbed the control. It was waiting
there for you. The motorman always kept his door shut
tight. he never intervened. the control was yours,
accessive to your touch like riverboat wheel
to countrylad who ran away from home.
It was all yours, whole hunks of articulated
car and engine. There was an extra window
for your pal, assistant motorman. You were thrown
to the very motion of darkness, but did not
enter. you saw the tumid waters but descended

not. here you are in command. Scateyeight
tons, and all yours. All that power—
and you *feel* it all—thrilling your arms as She verges

17

to start. Sidekick urges you on. Learn now
Mystery of wheel and axle along railcore,
Light-Eruption along infinite Track Circuit;
blur of the green aspect then the yellow
then the red aspect then the strange
milksnowy light that has no name and no
aspect at all at all

finally bringing Her home
in the white,
the heavy light
of train platform.   O

you can't   when   didit

          can't   didit

                    change when
the jolly conductor
                              turned scowly? when your skates got stuck
on the trolley track?
                              when the changebooth woman
had no change?
                              when they split the turnstiles
IN and OUT?
                              when did you start noticing
NO LOITERING signs
                              and stop noticing
the way backyard trees
                              hover between windowpot

                                        and clothesline?

2.

One morning I woke in the Beast and the Body of the Beast.
I woke but was still asleep in the waking that is indeterminate,
unconscient: In the morn that is neither morn nor eve in the dull
light that leaves only harrow.

Cloistered I woke in my dark and cloudy nature from whence
a certain vapor rises. I woke and was sullen in the very sweat of
my body, substance of the hard and the rude and the dark. The
Beast. And the Body.

I was awake in the radius of uniform color, surrounded as it
were with a flamelike bulb or envelope. I was the light that snares
the blood. I tasted the moist seed.

I searched for the jigsaw puzzle but could not find it. I wanted
to leave my flesh—but the Beast ensnared my body in Its Body. I
wanted to be in space, unfleshed, or in a place edging ever-outward
toward Otherness. The Beast held me in place. I was filled with
the Jealousy and the Wrath, the Weeping, Sighing, Moaning and
Lamenting, the Tearful Groaning.   *See*

> *that thou verge not down*
> *to the world of the dark rays*   black-rayed

> gloom-

        wrapped

I was awake in my accoutrements. Well-tonsured. But when
I walked to the 36th Street Station my teeth flared and my nostrils
fumed Animus. Beastcraw. I could feel the burn of the briefcase so
heavy in my hand. The graphs were scattering; the data was

19

haphazard. I couldn't go. I couldn't. They wanted me to, that whole crowd, pushing and shoving to Godzillaville. But the Beast was tapeworming my soul. I was in the Circle-Body. My eyes were heavy-laden, turned downward to nothing.

So I made a detour and went to the Hoyt Street station to catch the Number 2 IRT to fabled Flatbush, verylast stop. I yearned for the Heart of my youth. I wanted my pleroma, my freight railroad, the tennis courts they never finished near Avenue J. I wanted to waste that Beast and total the Body. I wanted to stash the briefcase but there was no time. When the Number 2 came—almost empty— who goes to Flatbush in the morn?—I put the briefcase in my lap and opened it. I was looking for my notebook, the one where I scribble lines in transit or gulping coffee in luncheonettes. Squiggly lines I can hardly read.

The notebook wasn't there. The graphs were sticking to their pouches; data was disbursed. That's okay. I was feeling gentler. The Beast was letting go my throat. I was respirating Anima. I could hear/see that noble array of stations, each to its proper rung, like milden rings in solar whirlpool. Could I remember?

    I did I did:

Hoyt (ah)
      /Nevens (out)
            Atlantic (breathe)/
                  Bergen /(in)
                  Grand Army Plaza (breathe)/
                  Eastern Parkway (ah)

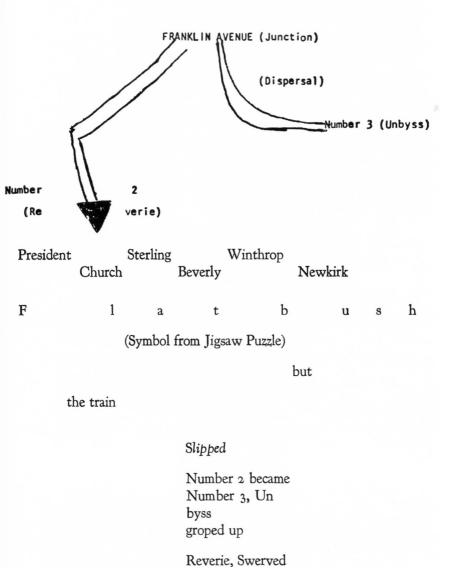

FRANKLIN AVENUE (Junction)

(Dispersal)

Number 3 (Unbyss)

Number   2

(Re   verie)

President   Sterling   Winthrop
    Church   Beverly   Newkirk

F   l   a   t   b   u   s   h

(Symbol from Jigsaw Puzzle)

but

the train

Slipped

Number 2 became
Number 3, Un
byss
groped up

Reverie, Swerved

into Animusmaw. Region aboveground but darker than tunnel,

21

yea, it is darkness, eternal dark
      ness   and not

           light. I
huddled within myself like that sullen figure sitting on a bench near
the prerevolutionary fort in the park that is not a park. It was into
that stretch between Franklin and New Lots they call The Beast,
most desolate on the System. The rails smoked in their stanchions.
Fire came into darkness. Rain seeped through the station tiles. It
belched and fumed out of railcore.

Then the voice of the conductor, disbursive, disembodied, as
an archon from some ghostly region, revealed the station-names and I
shook in their

strangeness and

raged in my shivering: Nos   trand

Avenue   Kings   ton

Avenue   Ut   ic   a

Avenue   Sut   ter

Sutter Avenue! stone's throw from my birthplace, castlehover
on Kings Highway and 98th And

it did it did

                 have red turrets. I could smell the urine
in the radiator. I ran to the window and saw

                                        and the head of

The Beast
                                is rubble and the eyes of

The Beast
                            are splintered wood and the mouth of

The Beast
                        is a wound of excavation and the teeth of

The Beast
                        are wanton rusty spikes and

The Body
                        is a vacant lot filled   (not
                                                      (with
                        with pulverized brick   (butterflies)
                        and shattered shatterproof
                        glass
                        and sprouts of
                        mattress-spring

                        and the limbs of

The Beast
                are exterminator fumes and the feet

        are the sewer-rats   *oh*

I saw The Beast on Sutter Avenue and my Heart broke with pain. *O
the weeping and groaning! O the tincture of metal and fire! O the wheel
of fierceness! O the fierce fire; torment and anguish! O the sharp pang
in the fire! O the sour, the bitter tears!* then It veered everdown to

N   e   w   L   o   t   s

23

(symbol from puzzle)

but there were *no* lots
only the dull false light that is neither light nor dark
cold fixed light of nether
ville
arcade-mutants whose husks contain

nothing ass

hole of the—

Hey, Buddy: that your B train?

THE PASSION OF EDWARD LUCIANO

At five o'clock in the morning, November 1, 1918, Edward Luciano became a Motorman. Sore-perplexed and grieving for the death of his little daughter only a week ago, Luciano was dazzled by this wonderment. But the Stationmaster explained that the Brotherhood of Locomotive Engineers (Motormen) had struck the BMT. So Luciano, BMT Dispatcher, became a Motorman at five in the morning. Control of the Culver Line Local was his.

Edward Luciano did not lack confidence. He knew the Culver Line, a slow level run along parks and cemeteries. Dispatcher was only one rung below Motorman. He knew the Track Circuit. And he knew the green aspect which indicates the signal blocks ahead are clear; the yellow aspect which indicates the next signal will be displaying a red aspect; and the red aspect which is a stop and stay indication. The bulbous wooden knob of the Control was strong in his hand.

At five in the evening, Edward Luciano completed his last run. As he pulled the Culver Line Local into the Ninth Street Station, he felt the Spirit of Death leave his body. Evening darkness reflected his fatigue. He had run the Culver Line for twelve hours without mishap. He was ready to go home. But the Stationmaster told him the BLE was still on strike and he would have to complete one final run as Motorman on the Brighton Beach Local-Express from City Hall all the way down to the Shore.

Edward Luciano shivered for his passion. The Brighton Local-Express was the trickiest line on the System, astounding even the highest-grade Motorman with its rollercoaster peaks and valleys, its switches and hairpin curves. Most perilous was the approach from Franklin Avenue to the Malbone Street Tunnel in Flatbush, hissing S-curve like Uroboros carved in its Circle-Body. Loop-de-loop the Track Circuit dipped from elevated to street level, lurching sharply to the right about twenty feet from Tunnelmouth, then veering sharply left less than fifty feet away.

As he entered the cab of the Brighton Local-Express with night falling on, Luciano saw an ad above the front window: TRY GRAPE NUTS. THE FOOD YOU'VE HEARD SO MUCH ABOUT. He shut the cabdoor and touched the Control with grudging hand. But when the train ground onto the bridge, and he pulled in safe at the Sands Street Station, his confidence returned. He turned the Control on high at the Franklin Avenue approach.

Control was his; he was braking and deciphering, moving brisk and bright among the green and the yellow and the red aspects. But as the train dipped down toward the Malbone Street Tunnel, he could see only the strange smoky light that is really no color at all, but is only texture, and this texture is of dried milk. And the smoky milklight took on a Goddess-aspect, folds of Anima, the hem of Her gown touching railcore, filling with Her Milk-Form the Tunnelmouth. So entranced was Edward Luciano by this Goddess who would receive the burden of his passion, he did not see the yellow light reflecting a sign: SIX MILES AN HOUR; he was doing forty-five . . .

Too late

he saw the Goddess become The Beast in the aspect of Her Milk-Texture; he was in the hissing belly of the Circle-Beast; he saw a Child's Face with sleepless smudge-eyes—then plunged

to Abyss.

when Edward Luciano awoke from his passion he was sobbing in the arms of his wife. O the sour groaning, the hard grieving, the dark tears! Miraculous Luciano's front car had held to the rails—but the trailing cars jumped the track. Dead were 97 or 102; injured 250. The crash shorted out the Third Rail Circuit. Electricians in the BMT powerhouse revved up the juice—electrocuting dozens of evacuees in the eerie smokelight.

26

Awaiting trial (he was convicted of manslaughter) Luciano learned the BMT would provide all signals with an automatic train-stop to insure proper observance of the stop (red) indication of the signal and that Malbone Street would be rechristened

Empire Boulevard

Reverie 14

Afterward

the child awakes
in his room
above the courtyard. Afternoon. Time

for milk. In his dream—
the shudder
dream receding to dream
time—Mother brings the cooling

glass. he feels the texture
thicken his tongue then
dissolve to moisture. feels

that space
not quite reverie neither dreamtime
to wander

anyplace   anytime

haphazardous   disarrangement

non
exitous   to no

where
so he leashes
Fido and they go
this afternoon without season
to streets where salsa
echoes
and pennants
left behind from
Sunday's block

                              party
      scour the breeze—

      comes to
                    Schoolyard
                                    playground; locked; in vain
Fido nuzzles iron-
                    spiked gate,
                                then droops his tail . . .
With smile of milden
                    gentleness the child
                                    pats Fido's
ear, then leads him along
                          strange
                                    triangular streets way
out on the wrong
                    other side of town
                                    to where compound
of an abandoned carnival
                          spills out
                                to shadow of an El
            in midst of
                    dismantlement.
                                on carousel
he lifts Fido to mane
                    of horse dappled brown-
                                    and-white, hovering
            still in perpetual
                          afternoon—
                                    the child mounts

horserump then rides,
                    with Fido as rein,

                                        that endless space
between reverie and dream
                          anywhere   to

                          anytime   Sun

        hover
                    s   Joshua

                                                        ly
as child dis
                  mounts giddy from motion that is as it
      were ever
                        still—hearing
the snap of ball
                      against bat
he leashes Fido
                      and they go,
                                  skirting monumental

                      cementblocks gouged
                      from El supports.

Earnest the child leans
                          toward baseball resonance
                                          but Fido leads
          elsewhere,
                      dallying down streets

      behind hat and pencil
                          factories
                                      hemmed

by pebble-shadow,

DEAD END signs. But Fido

finds a way:

        dirtpath between hedge and factory-wall

so narrow

        only child or animal

                could sneak through. Exitpath

        ends in thicket, shadow-

          wood,

            only to unshroud

unexpected entrance

        to a vast cemetery

            rurally extending

o'er beckoning undulate hills, leavings

            of the terminal moraine.

        cascading

          (lacustrine)

            skiffing

Sun

      to a height where bay and ocean
      converge below
      as if afroth from tiny blue craters

where whitecaps frolic.

       Miracle!

        at heart of Urbanville!,

vast rural

      cemetery!

        Enmarvelled

          the child

            yet frowns:

     the sign:

       NO DOGS ALLOWED:

so he gate-leashes Fido

                              and with a sigh—
                                        Fido vexed yet docile—
makes his way
                    among the living lower orders,
                                        the human dead.

Tiny flags and candles,
                              ribboned bouquets
                                        set round meek grave
            stones at first enlist
                                        his gaze. then notices

Lake intact with lilypods
                              faroff in russet haze,
Lilylake surrounded by
                              crypts. wandering again
in his world of besetting
                              wonderment, he finds a path
strewn with larchneedles
                              heralded

by thrushes, plumpy-brown,
                              and plump brash
                                        starlings.   by lake's
edge he sits
                    ever-fixed
                              in that space between reverie
            and dream. Crypts,

                              too,
clump in dream-mirage
slightly above hillocks,
mere reflection on
                    wavering water-surface. at far edge

of his mind
                gravemass is consigned;

                                        now thrives
the living world in ripe

                        ning dispensation. burns
within the lilybud

                        the yellow flowerheart, wombed
in nourishing white

                        filament like butterfly

                                        wing. lily

pods   in choiring   unison
    bend   in the   wind

                like ritual worshipper seeking Univocal,
                yet swaying in variant voices

                                        to the sky;
                on either side
                        of lakeshore

                                        auricular

                                beeches
                        weep down
                weep down
        sway down ever

                                        asway;
                        there joined in ovular array
        by willow, weeping mulberry;
        all trees in the cemetery
        yield to that sunheart of water,
        incline their leafy buds in measure
        equal to the lilypods.

Child amazed: regards
                    at lakecenter
                              a spur on a log
          magicalize to heron;
                              then come

brant, wild duck,
                    coot and bittern,
                                        Canada geese—
          none of these
                    can he name
except by sound and sight;
                    these suffice. enough
                              the bounding
          of wing and beak
                    adowning

all all
          Lilylake;
                    adfixation
                              of ruffled
                              breast
                                        to riffle
          of whirlpool—
                    and from internal
          hillforest

          where darkness
                    rises from empty vaults
                    where leaves bramble
                    and thicken and curl
                    as formidable
                              barrier

strange whirf and caw
                of creatures
                         unnameable   ever
        unknowable
                invade his introspection

as from an alien mode
                investing distance
                        to the locus
          of immediate attention. here
          the child would like to stay, place
          of endless afternoon, open
          eternal space of time's

          dissolution, un
          incessant
          ly un
          be

                coming . . . but
                    in one sour moment
                                of distraction
   Space subtracts itself
                and into timeless

Afternoon
        is bound
              (out of
                    Voidspace) breathy
          shroud of darkness.   Lilypods shiver and divide
               in dour contention. Lake surges
        to irregular whitecaps; tree-images blur
           in wind and the wild gusts
     send birds askim to sky entirely void

38

              of color. the child thinks of Fido
         leashed to exitgate   tear brims his eye.
                   to the gate

he is drawn—but then espies
                         a path where buckeyes
                                    loom on either side
like mute warders
                   guarding mossy stumps,
                                clumps of goldenrod
and purple aster. It is
                   the path to the crypts.
                                how can the child resist,

         now that afternoon is past,
                         such pathway to the dead?
Serious, self-resolved—
                   yet fey and jaunty (for he is but
                                         a child)—

he skips among the greeny mausoleums, the vaults
and sarcophogii, ledgergraves and catafalques. Inspects,
under the gaze of graveyard statuary, the lidless eyes,

tombs of sturdy limestone, weathered brownstone,
marble stately yet decomposing in the elements.
Almost alive but playing statue seem the caryatids,

bearing Greek columns with restraint;
gargoyles with batwings, angels
everkneeling, cherubs in flight. he traces

on each tomb the mural of a life
embedded on each loved one's heart as if
mirroring the stone. no metaphors of strife

are chiselled here; only peace;
they are never dead; they sleep.

grave upon grave, scroll upon scroll
they go to their long home

>   or join
>   seraphs and kin
>   in heaven. Even
Fido
     finds a place
>   reclining in noble
marble form
>   among the poplars. the child
still utterly alone
>   in whileaway maneuvers
now is drawn
>   to tiny grave set apart on green
mossy knoll:
>   PRECIOUS LITTLE GEORGIE
>   and writ in scroll:
Under de s'adow of Dy wing.'

no seraph flutters here,
>   no angels kneel,
>   no gargoyles peer.
unadorned

is Georgie's stone;
>   no tales to tell, no carved ikon to
>   describe
his little life.
>   yet!

40

wonderment!

                under preserving glass

is Georgie's likeness

        shaped in marble pure as the day it was cast

some hundred years ago. tenuous

the child touches glass

        to see his thumbprints cloud and disappear

like breath

        in winter air.   through the clear

gravewindow

     he stares

        at Precious Georgie.   the face

there so serene:

     snowy curls adorn

          Georgie's head, dance

  and tease

      down to his

         milky cheeks.

under white lids

     the Orphan Annie eyes

  gaze at a world

     of blank and null

         but with such surprise

they go all all

     acrinkle crinkle

       with simple

          joy; Precious

Georgie's lips

    are flecked in poutish

        puckered smile, as if

  bemused by all presentiment

of sacred bliss.

For an instant
        he stands in that aeon
                where Time is passive, space

reflexive;   bark
       of Fido from afar
              reminds him of harbinging

dark; as he turns
       and hurries to the gate
              he spies the Lillylake

now shuddering for rain.
        Fido's wag and woof vouchsafe
                  child-embrace.

       through streets triangular
       they skip and frolic Evening's Thoroughfare
       all all the way home
       to their room

           above the courtyard,

Reverie 15

Mother, lead me not down
To the dark realms

Goethe, *Faust*, Part II

Nor

    must we enter there   ●   where

  we have been, where

              we must go   ●   nothing

impels

    where all is

          rust   *on a certain morn*
                        mooncrux

                        in a cloudy sky

      fall
     all
          through a universe

pierces the shell of all pleromas
each shell   petalled layer of a baseball
stitches then the horsehide skin
to the pure white woolen yarn
to the pure grey woolen yarn to the pure red rubber
then the pure grey rubber
layer and layer   coil on coil

finally to the inner cork center
which is dark and taut and reveals
         cer   only itself.   *tain*

a certain

45

morn
                        when the moon was ghostbrain
         in a funnely sky.   it is not of itself

                                        Decay, this rust
but a distant Shape of Fire condensed

                                            in rustflakes.

                                        Dark realms
where we belong but Mother

                                        protect.   **On**
a certain morn
when the moon became the sun
Came
          to a neighborhood
                        without name.   only the streets
had name.
                haphazard

                          skittery
                          Wayfinder
                    we can go any direction
we choose
          will be *right* direction
                                long as we choose without
Animus. angles intercept; DEAD END
                                seals us off. Glenwood Road
disappears into Flatbush then picks up at
                                Nostrand. Nostrand
              Xes Flatbush near Amesfoort
                                    then runs parallel
a mile or so down near the ocean. Ocean Avenue
is not the same as Ocean Parkway but both impinge on
                                        Flatbush. that's

okay, these Xes, these intercepts: turning
down any street we can find whole new neighborhoods
without name, even dark realms past
Foster long as Mothers
Mother, protect. Mother—your *forbidden*
oathed us to the mystery of strange churches,
skittery streets.   Oh Mother—tell
of the chiaroscuro without disturbance,
schoolyards alive with foreign children,
punchball games of endless afternoon, hopskotch
under a moon that comes before sundown! Mother—
do your turn: dance the chalk squares: take ten
babysteps may I no you may not five
umbrella steps yes you may put
the torch to Castle Frankenstein . . .

                                    dislocation

all our lives
                        invades our symmetry. we want to drop
our masks, stash our gnostic guises, resist
all magick and alchemie.
                        Try

and nausea waylays us;
bowels turn queasy;
notebook smudged by the spilled coffee
of truckroute luncheonette;
pencilspoors all squiggly in

                        decipherable. On

                a certain morn
                when the moon bled
                in a factory sky

Came
to a neighborhood

without name. You'll start
vertical on Water Street (to
get here) or horizontal along Jay
or diagonal on Front—wherever

you'll wind up here, corner of Water and Dock. Of all you must
describe,
this is *most* indescribable: you don't want to—but you'll go:
to leave a spark, a bit, a particle in the
Unknowable. Turn one way, you'll see a swank river cafe
they come across the bridge for, those slumlords from Godzillaland—
'you will have a noble and *near* view
of the city'—remnants of a once-prosperous harbor,
the empty tollbooth where the tory lady informer saw the rebs

sneak across the river by nightfog. No one turns the other way
toward the Navy Yard, once neighborhood of seafood joints
for welders and dockworkers, tattoo parlors for sailors,
honkytonks for both. It had its own tang and touch; contained
Itself. then city planners got together with the men
who sell real estate. they shut down the Navy Yard,
extended the bridges for an expressway—drove the supports
right through the heart of this very *specific* neighborhood—

urban waste so bleak
you can't even call it ghetto. Yet there is much to wonder at
here—if you turn that way—and you're
It. Wayfinder. Perpetual
you stand at the corner of Water and Dock
in a mode of dislocation, fists jammed in windbreaker. Such

48

stillness. just a hop skip from the swank river cafe
but they never come here. the prosaic silence

of rust does not entice them. you want to move
(but you stand) if you move
a pleroma bursts—time intervenes. even the great
tilting light of the harbor has the sour taste
of rust. rust
verystuff of EMPIRE WAREHOUSES rust thick as
platemetal. nothing is warehoused here. windows gothic-
arched—small knights in chainmail might sneak through—

sealed in rust panelling secured by rustspikes
castlehover
98th and Kings Highway far away far away
and it did it did have red turrets. Yet
not so far away. at the far end of Water Street
two or three blocks from the harbor
hulks the bridge support
most humingous castlehover ever

alien spacecreature crouching
for attack. and at the round center
under the huge gothic stone   dark
realms
reign   all
      light sucked out. everything here says   *Forbidden*
Sophia's room
              behind the window. you

were never here with Herbie or Jeannie
or a pal or a sidekick   you were never here   you
          were not allowed
                        in the hospital room.

Not so far away Yet
                    this is Anima too.
    wind comes up; stillness
                    crumbles; now

you move   and as you move   *into* it
        it is day it is morn   yet WARNING amber
flares wooden detours   it is day   yet streetlights blush
like halfmoons
                    moving into METAL RECLAIMING
COMPANY Empire-Fulton Ferry State Park—a park
of empty warehouses—see *there is no decay!*—never *decay!*
Look: broken hydrants water moss

at warehouse base! street signs droop for rain,
yearn upward for sun! auto parts are greening, greening
in the rust! fields of gum reinforcements—a harvest—
a whole *field* of gum reinforcements
like the pyramids of grapefruit
only grapefruit in the window
of Teddy Trias' father's restaurant—then a whole

field of metal looseleaf fasteners!   *exhaled*
from the earth itself into the air above   you
want to go fast   you are going too fast when the whole idea
        is to go slow   you want to rearrange
whole neighborhoods
                    fix the rim
of the basketball hoop
so inner city youths can hit the periphery jumper pass

off the dribble juke and jive and do
the hesitation   *showtime*
                    you want to buy them uniforms

50

                    you want to go to The Commander's house
you want the trolley tracks to tootle
with trolleys carting warehouse goods
or at least go
              somewhere

not stop at FOUNT OF GOLD
AUTO REPAIR shambling into
seaman's church—oldest on the island some say—
Hudson and Front
where the striped pole
still twirls in front of the vacated barbershop. this is not
Ann Greener's church neat tuliprows and hedges (red

maple)
it is not the church of Dutch farmers or Suchachev villagers
or + BETHEL BAPTIST CHURCH on Nevens and 3rd,
stomping and swaying univocal welling up one
              Bessievoice.   Here only voices
of dead sailors.   once the weathered brick
shook with hymns from sea-shanty throats,

prayers for safe voyage.   now the ornamental iron gate
knocks in harbor-wind,
creaks with sound of ghosts   lock/spikes
drowned in rust.   bulletin board
is misadorned, stripped
a few ripped
pages of insane collage.   there is only
              the monument, always

              the monument:

IN MEMORY OF OUR BUDDIES
WHO GAVE THEIR LIVES
IN WORLD WAR II SO THAT
OTHERS MIGHT LIVE IN PEACE

please
let me go to The Commander's house
may I no you may not
visit The Commander   (hush)
rearrange

aeons   on

a certain
morn   it is

morn

and the windows of Cumberland Hospital
shine in moonglow

(yellow chalk)   (on sidewalk)

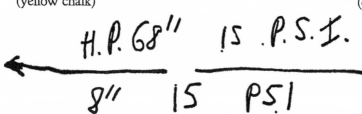

you move inland
on landfill

along Navy street

NAVY YARD
DEVELOPMENT
CORPORATION

has no develop

ment

      sly cat
      in the weeds
        muses
      for mice

      Marine Walk
      has no
          marine *life*

      glass

            bits

                inlap

shards

      of moon and sun

you want to go to the end
of COASTAL DRY DOCK to where glitters
a slight moisture
but this is WARNING/RESTRICTED AREA

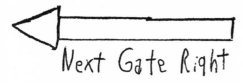

Next Gate Right

and GOVERNMENT PROPERTY is secured
by a guard in khaki uniform
      yellow badge
flow open for black official limousine
    but you, Way

          /official
          striped gates

        finder, must not TRESPASS
        you lack
        the black stamp
        on your wrist,
        identification
        bracelet, tattoo

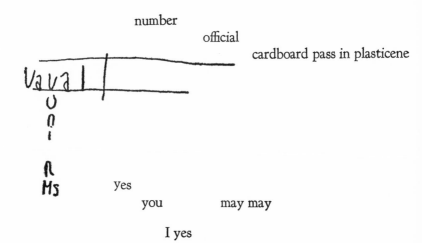

number

official

cardboard pass in plasticene

yes

you   may may

I yes

you may

go to The Commander's House   Twas

a sunny day in eighteen-ought-six
The Commander's House was done—
On a scree o'erlooking mated rivers
And ample fields of rustical flavor
Where gay beasties roamed.

Have you been to see The Commander
With peaked cap so white
O The Eastern Seaboard Commander
Whose eyes are hawkish bright?

Of handhewn oak in Colonial wise
The Commander's house was framed—
Trimmed in craftily carved mahogany
Adjoined with oakpins or handwrought iron
Exempt from rust or stain.

54

Have you been to see The Commander
    His braids are sparkly gold
O The Eastern Seaboard Commander
    With gaze so fearsome bold?

        A chandelier of beaten bronze adorned
            The Commander's Oval Room—
        Under wicks of intricate Grecian form
        Exotic Admirals and Ladies dined
            And did the cotillion.

Have you been to see The Commander
    His House is Quarters A—
O The Eastern Seaboard Commander
    Who holds all ships in sway?

        Elegant pyramids of cannonball
            Graced The Commander's lawn—
        A marble column for the seamen twelve
        Who gave their lives at the Barrier Forts
            In Old Canton.

Please take me to see The Commander
    So crisply straight-o-spine
O The Eastern Seaboard Commander
    With shoes of inky shine.

        Like a silken seraph in Wall'bout Bay
            Sailed The Commander's yacht—
        From his private porthole he might survey
        The kaleidescope of Naval Yard Ways,
            The buzz of busy docks.

I'll take you to see The Commander
    And his Shore Patrolmen too
O The Eastern Seaboard Commander
    In duds of Navy blue.

                Maps and globes and compasses and quadrants
                    Filled The Commander's dreams—
                From his snug aerie off Hudson and Front
                Deployed with chalk and tiny shipmodels
                    The Invincible Fleet.

So you've been to see The Commander
    His Vigilance is deep
O The Eastern Seaboard Commander
    For your sake never sleeps   Now

                But where   (Nor enter there)
        is our Commander   where O
            where has he gone be   gone
this morn when the moon is a blister

                                            in a sky of horn
            The Commander is gone
for good
                they took down the portraits in the entranceway

of all the Commanders
        since Jonothan Thorne (1806)   and The Commander's
                                                House an empty
            ghostrealm
                        and the Oval Room is still—
though some say on gay mild nights
                            you can still hear (fiddles
                and celli faint) laughter of Admirals and Ladies
                    as if in ghostdance

under the bronze chandelier—

and the caretaker of The Commander's House
in his modest woodabode adjoining
caretakes

nothing

but stray coupling
dogs   and The Commander's House

o'erlooks

rusting
water towers
funnelblack   Con

Edwaste   BOERUM AND PEASE

BLANK BOOK
AND
SHEET METAL
DEVICES

devices

dee

vices

yet

there is no decay   never

decay   Navy Yard

will bloom, will bloom again, fair seedtime
in its flowering!

Docks
whence the Monitor, dark-turreted, scudded south to tryst

57

iron-ribbed Merrimac—
where Battleship Maine and Superdreadnaughts Iowa
and 'Mighty Mo' were launched—
these Ways and Docks will trans
mogrify to CLICK Industrial Park!
huge Godzillacranes will batter EMPIRE WAREHOUSES—
rust will mushroom up
up in furious gusts
to the very outer rungs!—and from waste places
will rise FULTON LANDING LUXURY TOWER APTS!
yea—they will repair the broken hydrant, straighten street
signs, clear out auto parts!
Ground-breaking ritual! Ceremonial driving of the first spike!
Ribbon-cutting! City cronies! Borough moguls!
a National Guard drillteam will prance where once the Navy
band marched—O The Commander's pride!—
those swell white uniforms, gold braid and buttons, sun-
embossed horns!
                                        Hey

                                    we'll be there
alright, me and Herbie—
                        and Jeannie!
                                        Remember
                Oh Mother
                        Remember:

We are Nature too

Reverie 16

Gonna kick your ass all the way to Canarsie

You wan' pizza or hamburger?
Canarsie mother to her son

And the Indian shed a tear like child
            leashing Fido to the gate to wander Lillylake. the Indian
Canarsie
                  Indian, our Twin so close yet other. Twins
we were redcheeked   sun /androgynous moon before
bigmacher tore
                        asunder. Twin so close so
Other.   pal
Alright
            sidekick from way back when (didn't we spot him
on the B62 bus?)
                        he was sitting at the time
we never came here
            why would we ever   he was sitting at a booth

                  in Seaview Diner in Canarsie
rolling his own and drinking java black and hot
freshbrewed in the pot like they knew to make for him it would
                                    sear
another's tongue. at the time he was examining, The Indian,
a discarded notebook he picked from a rusty trashcan still firing
                                    trying
to decipher another's discursive notation. he was watching the
                                    buses
pass on Seaview Avenue from Starrett City to Gravesend Bay.
                              Starrettity
hovering in gloomy terraces awthwart the sky
            across the plains stone

                                    turrets of Gravesend Bay
        he shivered   he was in a swoon
                                    The Indian

        turned his back and thought he saw the exterminator laying
                                                down rat poison
        near the kitchen door of Seaview Diner. in the notebook
        he could make out only squiggles. on Seaview Avenue
        he saw a rainbow webbing out to iridescence between the
                                                            parking
        meters. maybe he was thinking
        in a dreamtime of pleromas
        in a spacetime of aeons
        how Canarsie ass
        hole of that Place that is ass
        hole of the Universe
        yet once was hameshe* was in desolation

        jutting out to bay and inlet,
                salt creek and basin. Canarsie: most western
    of those thirteen tribes spawning sparsely
                                    across the island.   hunting
                    rabbit on Barren Island   how
                        you can still find muskrat in the drained
    cattail marshes off the Belt Parkway
                                    across from Starrett City. they don't know,
                those guys fishing off Canarsie Pier fancying themselves
                        outdoorsmen. only he knows,
            The Indian and maybe
                                    those dune-squatters in spile-shacks
    shucking polluted oysters off Fresh Creek (or it is reek! o it is sour!)
                                                                Basin

*homey

                                62

                              No
                    we never came
          here who
                    would want
          to miles and miles of Flatland
                                        refuse devouring

        Itself
                    cattail shambling the horizon like devouring wheat
our own alien
                    prairieland   heartland
                    of heimarmene   where fires froth and fume per
                              Petual

                              No

                              No
                    too far it
          was too far a
                              toofar Place of
          odorous   mudflats   crushed
autohoods.
          we never came here on our rollerskates
          we never biked here No never played hooky
          here like sprawling in sedge of the railroad cut
          chawing on shucks and counting the freightcars
          like any hicktyke from oncerural
          America
                    though the streetnames were the same
          Glenwood   Farragut even dreaded
                                        Foster
              but they were darkening
                              the street
                              signs a mishmash of zig

                              63

                                    Zag
                                            striking down toward
heimarmene
                        Malingering
                                    Malevolent

                                                            Sea
                        mostest of the furth
                                                        est out
                        Place You never said
Canarsie
                        it was forbidden region
of gangland massacre
                                        so remote almost to forego
Forbidden almost a place
                                of end
                                            graves.
                                                    we
                never came here, heard
                tell of it from the men who told schoolyard epics; how
                it smelled of acrid chemicals and moldy apricots and burnt
                film; how you took the LL of all
                subways most austere, ascetic
ally assault
                        ive.
                                    first ferrising toward Godzillaville,
                                                                skirting
                those cleaving monuments,
                                            then rollercoasting through a
                                                            graveyard
                to the end line. It was uncontainable it had no

                        Limit
                                The Indian

                                    64

                he knew he knew and no one else
Cept the squatters an
                                illegal/fugitive
                                                or two
                        this region once knew a perfect childhood childhood
                a perfect day
The Depth   of Silence/   Mother lost   Silence the noises
                                        when leaves of the white oak

        were large as a mouse's ear
        Crow came with a grain
        of corn in one ear, bean
        in the other   tail
                of beaver, pumpkin

                                                seed
                                                how
                coppermouth is tamed in the cattail (you
bite off his head)
                        At night may I roam, against the wind may I roam
                        When the canoe is boating may I roam
                        At dawn may I roam, against the wind may I roam
                        When the crow is calling

        may I roam   may I roam   yes

                        you may   Thunder, Perfect Mind

        and roam this whole vast island
        thrusting Atlanticward like a sort of Crete
        in the middle of the sea, edge
        of a continent middle of all there is. Dance
        in garments so feathery they 'shed rain'
        like eagle-feathers. Glide
        in your Canarsie fishing canoe

                                65

made not of flimsy bark but of pine or chestnut
for rough waters of the Sound/the great salt Bay,
forty feet long without mast or sail
and not a nail in any part. Even then
they had the taste and the tang
of this Place that makes chimeras. Comes

ship carrying big white wings,
strange bird from the sky or Ocean-monster. Miss Harrison
tells us it's 1609 and a sailor from the *Half Moon*
has set foot on the tip of Coney Island. Canarsie
kills him. They sell Manhattan Island to the Dutch
and they don't even own it. Are they a line of Delaware,
Algonquin or Mohican? What is their lingo? How
did they get the name? Miss Harrison doesn't know.
Maybe they saw the fenced gardens of Dutch fur traders

and called the land *Canarsie*—"the fenced land"—
giving themselves a name not their real
name which might have been *Keskachene*
having something to do with level grasses. Maybe
—it says this on the jigsaw puzzle—it comes from the French
"canard," Duck being the Keskachene totem. Whatever

he sure kept getting
                    fenced: 1665: Canarsieland
                    deeded to the Dutchtown of Flatlands
                                    (New Amesfort)
for 100 fathoms of wampum, one coat, one pair of stockings,
one pair of shoes, four adzes, two cans of brandy, half
a barrel of beer:
                    'Wanetappack, Sachem of *Canaryssen*
'and others named lawful owners of Canaryssen and the
                                    appendages thereunto

'appertaining—sold to the inhabitants of New Amesfort—a
                                                    parcel of land—
'with conditions that the purchaser once for always
'a fence shall set at *Canaryssen* for the protection of the
                                                    Indian-cultivation,
'which fence shall thereafter by the Indians be maintained
'and the land enclosed by the fence shall by the Indian-owners
'above-mentioned
                    all their lives be used . . .'

The English gave him 'libertie to fish in convenient places
'for shells to make wampum . . . also
'they are to have the finnes and tayles of all such whales
'as are cast upp . . .'   but
                                                hush

                    he got a regular fencejob

The Indian

                    like everything *is*

                                        a voice

                    Canarsie:
                                        Enemies: Eskimoppas

and his Rockaway; raccoon-greased
Iroquois, tall crafty Northerners
swoop down for tribute:
and in no time—what-lament
of eaglebone flute—no time
                            atall (1830)

            Jim de Wilt ("Jim the Wild Man") **last**

Canarsie *in* Canarsie is found
        coldstone dead in his shack off
Paedergat Basin and Mrs. Anthony Remsen *the*

Dutch society Mrs. Remsen sews him his

                                      coffin

                                           shroud . . .

                  where   what

                                  where the music

to express?

                      we want to

               scour

                      the need, erase

                            the poem, staunch

        the music. why? because
everything got Canarsied, fucked, fenced and
Canarsied: it simply wanted

                        its own taste and tang
and it got it
                Canarsie

Baymen
        haul the rich fish harvest, flounder, snapper, blue,
        oystermen nurse oysters like starfish, clamdiggers
        work the beds in a swoon. So
City Fathers
        build their incinerators here,
        burn garbage all down the beach
        from Fresh Creek to Paedergat Basin,
        seal the bay in the sour pollution. who wants
Canarsie clams?
        would you? they want to build an amusement park
        the villagers, to rival fabled Coney. no
        Steeplechase here, no Dreamland or Luna Park. not in

Youknowhat.

        they call it *Golden City*: rotting boardwalk
        on spiles along Seaview Avenue, an x-ray
                        machine, foot massager,
        miniature steam engine, Esmerelda the Fat
                                        Gypsy

Fortuneteller.

        no one comes to Golden City—would you?—
        and you can't get here if you wanted
        except by boat from the Rockaways
        only a toonerville trolley in the immediate
        vicinity there is no subway yet
        so Canarsie is set off even from
        Canarsie. City Fathers
                don't get around to sewage. and Canarsie,
    knowing its own taste, shape
                        of mixture and dispersal

they brought the refreshing wind
and cast it into the scouring wind
                says: *Give me everything you don't want:*

        'Dump on dump on me
                some more.   Pollute
        my primal cattail with dense seed

        of refuse.   Pile crud
                on weeds over rags of crud.   Sting my belly
        sore with every manner of unobliterative turd

        and burn the refuse to a charring gel
                which chokes itself within its
        spaces.   O please no surcease from the blech

69

of incineration!   let the black fires
       curl against a shut sky as from nostrils
of raging Beelzebub!   Pismire

make of the salt smell
       of my beaches   so that the puff
of once-reviving Seabreeze sickens and wilts

and pains.   Now rough
       me up with gangbang: bring garbage disposal
plants, bone-boiling shops, fish oil

factories.   ship here dead animals
       for fertilizer.   You, Lepke
Buchalter, emerge from Brownsville

with your felt hat, your soft scarf, your spiffy
       camel's hair.   and you organize
your Murder Inc. and dump your blownout mangled
                              bodies

here in my bowels, my core where thrive
       the tools of rot. Maybe
just the butchered parts   maybe the yegg entire

so the trough of separation inweaves
       with protoplasmic ooze.   then roll
the whole sloughy

mes   meric   metamesom
       orphic fudge into a smell
so incarnate of Shape and Form

as to reek of Uncontainable
       ness.   Dispirit

is my Name "handy hamlet
on which to hang a gag, the place
that is nowhere, the end of the line."
                                    Yet even You,
                                            Canarsie,

are not abandoned. You
have your Village. Village
of perfect childhood. Italian
illegals, alien
from way back, tougher
even than Lepke-roscoes
find your meadowlands somehow
for vineyards and fruit trees, truck farms for lettuce,
beans, tomatoes and even some 'big stuff'
corn and spuds.
                            We too

            would want
                            Our
            Selves
                        a Village to
saunter to,
                    shape and sally of
it, sashaying
                    to Western edges. Village
where the statues have eyes and nod
wisely (un
            Orphan Annied)
caryatids step down from gravestones and
on meadows flutter almost fleshly.   here
                                    in yestersurge
                                    before we merge
to Starrett City
an English painter on holiday

71

might sketch us as cavorters by woodframe houses,
raffers of tooning goats, warders
of pigeoncoop, rabbit

                hutch.
                          here we are
                     and how did we ever
                get here
where we said
                never to go.   on Conklin Avenue
shards of Village
             remain.
             Canarsie Dutch Reformed Church
tarries in white plankwood,
                 stoics cloudward
                              its New England spire.
a cemetery of birdnests
                and broken stone—
                          air's hint of forest,
sparrows
        in a churchbush—one jay
                      in one bare tree—
might be enough
          of the natural world
                   somewhere between Otherness
and that Other
        Place.
            Cemetery
               relapses
to Garbage Dump
        but the pigeons nestle here and one
                     snowy gull.
Canarsie Cemetery
      might be real country

                                  for someone who has never known real
country.
                    Church
                              Lane   farmhouses

remain
              upsurge
                        of leaves
                                    bring
                                          reverie
                                                      merge
Village a
                    brueghal
Ann Greener
                    little blonde Dutchgirl
                                          scooting ducks
with quilted apron
                    or skating on Fresh Creek,
                                              Paedergat Basin
red scarf
          ascrawl
                    red lips ruddy
red cheeks.
                    but oh so soon so
very soon, in a
                    swoon—what—space   *The Pigeons*
of junkman
                    tune—breath   *of Canarsie*
                    in winter air
                    flicked
gaze through clear
                    gravewindow—

                                              on rooftops
                                              conspire

73

one sour moment
                    of distraction—Village
slouches—Miss Harrison, you gave us history's
lesson—to Starrett
                    City: it was false
Village, Village of the False Light. like in the spy film
where the Village is really a camp for lobotimized ex-Interpolers
and the pink fountain disguises a cellar of bleak cots   picture
postcard stageset carnival
dismantled on the outskirts and the refuse
left behind.   Starrett

City Starrett   CityStarrettCityStarrett
                                        City: O the sound
                                        of it, roll of it
        on the tongue!
                        on the LL
                    hovering from New Lots all down to Broadway
                                                        Junction
        final zone of
                    Ringalevio: how long
                    you have been here with us, fractioning
our dreams in the building,
rising smoothly from these flatlands
your flat beige rectangles
your topless towers, Babylonish
seven-wonderment   upsurge
thrill *upward*   tumesce
                            to Canarsie sky!

                            we can't saloogi
        you and we don't want to. if you are Darkness
        we must pollute ourselves in you
        to gain the light. if you are Light

74

you are more than
                         Mirage.

                                    At Night

when you rise electrically in your compartments
out of the sea-engirdlement
you are Luna Park, Acadia, Alexandrian
                                              light-beacon!
O we must know
                         the sealed-in security
                         of your immense rectangles
                         total experience of living
                         with every modern convenience
                         including special buses to the
                         subway a private police force
                         swimming pool and rec
                         area even our own public school!

You are pure
             plenitude of Where; Thereness
Absolute.
                 but how do *we* get *there*?   where
is
       Access?   edge

along the Belt Parkway
                            where Indian Trail remnants
                  with primeval cattail, sumac and scrub pine
                  (smell of sea mixed with urine)

                       cut off from Starrett City by quonsetshapes
           moulting in the sun
                          pickup trucks in the wrecking   stoop

to Canarsie Pier
                    where scarcefew enter
            save archons in windbreakers and mackinaws
            hands stuffed in pockets
                        or displayed in torn mittens
            fingers stick through
                        and we're only far
as the wire fence
            of a water pollution plant. So
            here's what we'll do: scoot left

            away from the bay
                        we can't get to

            anyway
        we'll skip and scoot
        like skipping only on the black
    duck the cars in a swoon
                        and enter under the arches of

76

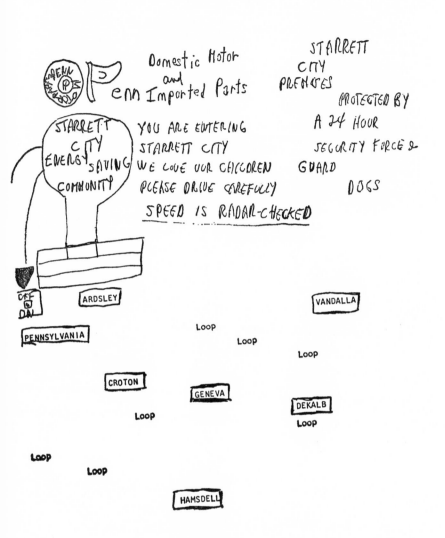

Domestic Motor
and
Penn Imported Parts

PENN

STARRETT
CITY
PREMISES
PROTECTED BY
A 24 HOUR
SECURITY FORCE &
GUARD
DOGS

STARRETT
CITY
ENERGY SAVING
COMMUNITY

YOU ARE ENTERING
STARRETT CITY
WE LOVE OUR CHICDREN
PLEASE DRIVE CAREFULLY

SPEED IS RADAR-CHECKED

CAT
DIN

ARDSLEY

VANDALLA

Loop

Loop

Loop

PENNSYLVANIA

CROTON

GENEVA

DEKALB

Loop

Loop

Loop

Loop

HAMSDELL

77

we
foot pilgrims
with Ozlike hearts
and breath
like Tarsus bells
would enter you

                    Starrett
                    Starrett
                    Starrett

                City

but you give no

                    Access
                there is no inner to your outer
                you have no inner core
                only the outer shell of

                        Hoverhusk

WALDBAUM'S   Lou's Audio Post
  SHOPPING   RED APPLE RENT-A-
                              CAR

                    Carvel's   McCrory's
                Pumpernicks's   Deli   May We
MALL   Shampoo Your Garments Ice Cream Cakes
            for all occasions

        Your North is House of Auto Wreckers
        Your South is Ghostsmell of Garbage Dump
     Your East is 26th Ward Pollution Control Plant

78

Your West is Shroud-of-Darkness
we cannot enter you we cannot escape you you cannot escape

Canarsie.

The half past 9 a.m. train on the Brooklyn and Rockaway Beach Railroad is leaving East New York for Canarsie. For a pleasant and economical trip, commend us to this trip to the seashore.

The fare to Canarsie is 15 cents on the cars. In the summertime, and in pleasant weather, the open excursion cars are used, and in the warmest weather, a delightful breeze sweeps through them laden with the perfume of the wild flowers in the woods which skirt part of the way or with the invigorating air of the salt marshes, over which the latter part of the trip carries us.

The cars are drawn by an engine making little smoke or noise. The track is level: we saw no cut deeper than three feet and no embankment to tumble over.

There is a novelty about the trip that is refreshing. The strip of land belonging to the railroad company is so narrow as to look like a lane running through the woods and meadows, occasionally passing through someone's potato patch or corn field and intruding upon the dooryards of the few dwellings on the route.

The steamer "Carrie" leaves Canarsie 10:30 a.m., 1:00 p.m. and 3:00 p.m. The fare is 30 cents, and in about half an hour we are landed at any one of the shores of the Atlantic, where billows beat incessantly on the pearly sand.

We found Mr. B.F. Judkins, superintendent of the railroad, a quaint gentlemanly man, who evidently knows how to manage a good road and how to please the public. We never saw a railroad train before where all the passengers seemed not only not inclined to grumble, but decidedly pleased with all the incidentals and minutae of the trip.

Reverie 17

One late Saturday afternoon of a hot summer's day in a land without climate (wasteland of space, wilderness of time) me and Herbie went to the Century movie theater on Nostrand and Flatbush.

For a long time we stood by the candy counter trying to make up our minds. Herbie chose Goobers and I chose Raisenettes. They had no Coke machines then. We drank from the white porcelain water fountain in the loge.

Saturday afternoon then was mothers and fathers and kids. It was a lot of noise and kids running down the aisle chasing Spaldeens. But we picked an inbetween show when most of the kids were mobbing out.

Back then they didn't turn the lights on between shows or even play any music. The aisles had no carpets. An usherette in a white uniform showed us to our seats with a flashlight. We hunched in our seats and crunched our Goobers and Raisenettes and put our feet up on the empty seats in front. The theater was dark except for the red EXIT sign and the quantiful white light from the projectionist booth way above us.

It was an inbetween show but they still ran the serial. They skipped the cartoons but we didn't care; we were too big for that. Last week was the last Boston Blackie chapter and this week was the first Captain Midnight chapter. Paul Kelly was a reporter on an afternoon daily but he was also Captain Midnight fighting The Gang that was strangleholding his city and The Law powerless to appre-hend. They called him Captain Midnight because when he changed from his alter ego to his Main Man he wore an inky black costume with cape and hood dark as midnight.

In this first chapter Captain Midnight did some truly marvelous things. He accosted The Gang in a diamond warehouse and dodged machinegun bullets they were shooting down on him from a balcony. He jumped on top of a massive crate, grabbed a cargohook, swung himself up over the balcony railing and knocked over seven members of The Gang. Before they had time to recover he tossed all seven gangsters over the railing into a pool of wet lime. Most incredible of all he ducked the pistolshots of two mobsters standing at pointblank range—you could see bullets punch into a cratebox behind him!

But in the end The Gang overpowered Captain Midnight. The seven roscoes got out of the limepool and grabbed him as he was ducking bullets. It took all seven and the other two but finally they blackjacked him unconscious, tossed him in the trunk of a Packard and drove him to their hideout, a huge cave in the country. The Big Boss was there in his underground shelter waiting for Captain Midnight, surrounded by all the comforts of home: radio, record player, Waring blender. He was waited on by young women in shimmering gowns who carried tapers. Unlike the underlings, who were most uncouth and spoke lowlife underworld lingo, the Big Boss was a Genius. He was cultured and well-educated and spoke with an uppercrust British accent. When they brought in Captain Midnight, the Big Boss was sitting in a fancy robe salting soft-boiled eggs.

The Big Boss didn't waste much time with Captain Midnight. He nodded and ate his soft-boiled eggs with a dainty spoon. The mugs took Captain Midnight to a conveyor belt at the end of which was a huge electric buzzsaw. Before they turned on the conveyor belt, one of the gang activated the buzzsaw and splintered a huge chink of pinewood. They left on the buzzsaw and turned on the conveyor and Captain Midnight was transported headfirst to certain doom.

That was the end of Chapter One.

For a few moments the theater was quite dark except for the red EXIT sign. Then the main feature came on. I don't remember the name. It had John Garfield and Ida Lupino and Akim Tamiroff played Ida Lupino's father. I don't remember much about the film—not the way I remember Captain Midnight. It was scary in a kind of inacessible grownup way. Garfield and Lupino were lovers. Garfield and Tamiroff were in some illicit traffic together smuggling or bootlegging or gunrunning and Tamiroff didn't want sweet daughter Lupino to know. Much of the action took place at night on small shoreboats somewhere between the Narrows and Coney on what might have been Gravesend Bay. There was a lot of nightwind and spray and tarpaulin. I keep getting it mixed up with other John Garfield films where he's a boxer or Spanish Civil War leftist and they torture him in a bathtub by letting cold water drip from the faucet onto his forehead.

But the opening scene has stuck in my head—and Herbie's too. It's on a windy nightbeach. Fog. You hear surf breaking against shorerock kush kush kush. Closeup you see a dead body, fully clothed, face down between the breakers and the rock. You know it's a mobster: the camera shows you the cufflinks and the fancy pinky-ring still on his hand. Eddying nearby the silk scarf, the fedora. You think of the headlines where Murder Inc. made another hit and dumped the body on Canarsie Beach off Jamaica Bay.

After the movie it was still evening but it seemed like night. The sky turned loury. It was cooler. Herbie said let's stand here on the corner of Nostrand and Flatbush and take the first bus to the end of the line. I didn't want to—I wanted to go home—but I couldn't be chicken. About five different buses stop at the corner of Nostrand and Flatbush. We waited about ten minuues. The B16 was first to come. We sat in the back on the seat that goes across from hub to hub. There were few passengers: some hospital nurses, an old woman with a torn skirt and a surgical bandage on her bare right leg, a cop who got off at the first stop. The busdriver's pal sat across from him on the seat that goes catty-corner so he was looking at the driver's profile. He wore a light blue windbreaker, unzipped, and worked a toothpick. In the rearview mirror we saw the driver's black-peaked cap but his face was shrouded in darkness. From the way he fisted the big round clutch you could tell he was in command.

The bus slunk down Nostrand to Glenwood then down Ditmas. It varoomed on Ditmas zooming past the trees of Flatbush   (the thick-trunked, the luxuriant-leaved)   oncevillage of sanitaria and cloisters. It eased by Midwood High and P.S. 152. Islands of bush and granite sprouted from the middle of the road. It braked at Ocean Avenue and Ocean Parkway, broad thoroughfares of much traffic.

It stopped at an industrial park/market area on Ditmas and 18th Avenue. No one got on and no one got off. The industrial park was next to an old synagogue and next to the synagogue was a boarded up frame house. The structures melded into one. The small buildings, etched in silhouette, took on the darkness faster than the sky.

The bus stopped at 13th Avenue. All the people got off clutching their transfers like tatters in the wind. All that was left was me and Herbie and the driver's sidekick. It verged down 13th Avenue toward Fort Hamilton Parkway. We knew Fort Hamilton as a day-place with curving ample bikepath—you could really whip along the shore watching the big white ships scud on a sea that seemed to be almost respirating. But this was the nightbus: almost before we turned around: there was no dusk we could recall. All we could see out the window was our own faces, dim and strange, scattering with motion. The driver drove the clutch and the bus jolted all down Fort Hamilton Parkway to Gravesend Bay. This was the end of the line. We thought we heard the driver mutter "Gravesend Bay last stop" but we couldn't be sure. We stepped off the bus in a swoon. The driver and his pal stood in front of the dimmed headlights lighting cigarettes; they paid us no mind.

Now we were at the end of the line and we didn't know what to do.

Herbie said let's walk out on the causeway that juts into Gravesend Bay so we can be right there where the water breaks. I didn't want to. I was frightened—and Herbie too. I don't know why he said it. But we had to do it.

We were walking stone but we were also walking Gravesend Bay in the huge rockbasin where the water breaks. It was cold. There was always nightfog there. It rolled in soft as tumbleweed but twice as thick. The further we went the windier it got.

We heard the waves break against rock kush kush kush. We thought of the dead gangster face down in water, fully clothed. Our legs got heavy. We turned and ran back down the causeway to the waiting bus. The driver and his buddy were still in front of the headlights, smoking cigarettes. We ran onto the bus and hunched in the back seat, shivering. The driver got back on without his sidekick. He fisted the big round clutch and hummed the motor; the bus turned back down Fort Hamilton Parkway toward 13th Avenue. The bus never stopped; no one got on and no one got off. All the way home we were the only passengers—me and Herbie.

Reverie 18

Say

how are ya?

And watcha been doin'?

Did we lose the track and the touch of each other?

It was my fault maybe. I got bolluxed up with subway maps and
train schedules, xeroxes of memos and the other short shrift in my
briefcase. But there's still time. Always

in the dreamtime.

There's the freight railroad—remember?

We're in no rush. never. an idleness
of sorts, no edges or boundaries,
no safety net no network
of arrangements.
                he had his Falls, that Patterson
mythmaker
        to myth him to reverie
rock him in bosomy warmth,
swoon him to sleep.
                        we of bleaker
urbanwaste
        must seek and pick among inland rubble
and do it all without really seeking. we have to get lost or at least
be willing to get lost.

we think of you, freight railroad, gleaming like a frozeup swimming
hole down along Avenue H where it crosses Flatbush, near the
Century movie theater and the half-finished tennis courts, flanking

one-family bricks and the college athletic field. playing hooky

in endless afternoon
                          under shadetrees
                                            of the railroad cut
head against hard earth
chawin' weeds unnamable
                          countin' boxcars.
                                       It never went more than five
                                                    miles an hour
          Toonerville   tooner

          villesque
                     and it did and it did

use abandoned trolley tracks and subway tunnels.
hauled ashes from factories, rubbish from industrial plants to fill in
the Coney marshes for one-family bricks. hauled huge tonnage of
wine grapes for villagers to moonshine in cellars.
Before the regulators made them switch to diesels they used electric
locomotives like trolley cars with just a motorman's cab, trolley pole,
                                                                    mini

caboose. Diesels

were shifted front to back at subway tunnels to *push* the cars along
track. boxcars were parasitic: hand-me-downs from other freightlines
floated by way of Hoboken . . .

Do the freights run here anymore?

What do they haul?

                          Today

                          92

we're way too far from Avenue H. too far to walk,
        Slowmovers. Still
        we want to follow
        our freight railroad
        never leave it

behind. So we'll head out for the docks 39th near Bush Terminal free
as any kid kicking up cinders.   flanked
        by brown-spouting metal pipes
and tracks all scatter

                  /skelter

the engines
          are ever in repose,
            yellow caboose with black stripes, yellow

        cargocars.
               black-bearded
yardmen sit in loading cabs, smoking thick cigars, waiting
to load cargo onto lorrie dolls. but
where's the track   track skeltering done gone
to infinity.   we could ask directions
of that man in a yellow hardhat
but he might chase us away: are we supposed to be here?

Anyway it's fun hiding behind pipes until he disappears.

Look! it picks up again at 4th Avenue, gleaming like a street rainbow
laid end to end . . . then leaps away
from the construction workers

        disappears behind a stationhouse, this time
for good.
        we'll never

ever

find it, the end

of this freight railroad

            oh the freights
don't run here no more, say the people at bustops and kiosks,
they used to run along McDonald Avenue, but they don't
no more.

But look: if we backtrack to where we were: kids
shinny up shadetrees in the railroad cut,
caper in treehouses, stride along track and ties
among the torn tires, discarded

inner tubes. come on:

                  we'll crawl
                  over the embankment
                  sprawl
                  on hard earth
                  of a railroad cut
                  chaw on a weed
                  check out a wayward
                  gull.
                          then we'll shinny

up a shadetree
        slide down
                like on a greased pole. we want

that ole freight train oh we want to count boxcars

like hookydays off Avenue H. but that can happen
too
if we really want it. here she comes: out of the darkness
of a subway tunnel
arumble
but slow and almost genteel always
in low gear never
no rush.
         count   the boxcars (take

all the time you want)
            watch the placenames

      go by—Oregon, Ohio, Nebraska,
Santa Fe, Kansas City, Wabash, Topeka, Mobile, Kalamazoo—
placenames   oncerural America, feeling you belong
like Missouri Huck or Mississippi Slim or any
country rube.
      Look!
          red signal!
                She's idling
by a crossing: our chance to commandeer: you take the diesel you're
in control. Me
I'll be sidekick in the caboose. we've got on
our farmer overalls, our motorman caps. rev her up pal we'll
roister
clear crosscountry: leveltrack
be Iowa cornfield/Kansas
wheatfield   a rise
     be prairie   S-curve
Rocky Mountain
      canyon, High

        Sierra pass . . .

and we
never even

left home.